From the Playground to the Pulpit

--moving from a place of vulnerability to a place of strength

Lisa Gillespie

Kingdom Journey Press
A Division of Kingdom Journey Enterprises
Woodbridge, VA

ISBN-10: 0989087824
ISBN-13: 978-0-9890878-2-7

Printed in the United States of America.

Published by Kingdom Journey Press
A Division of Kingdom Journey Enterprises, Woodbridge, VA
www.kjpressinc.com

Cover Design by Elisha Speller, www.elishaspeller.com

Dedication

I would like to dedicate this book to the memory of my mother, Mrs. Thelma R. Anderson. She was truly the light of my life, my rock and my anchor until she passed me into the loving arms of God, who became all these things to me and more. Mom, I love you so much and I still miss you every day.

I thank God for giving me the strength and courage to be transparent enough to include all that is contained herein. I realize that much of what is discussed here will bring varied aspects of judgment and opinion from those who read it. However, I am happy to say I'm no longer worried about that. I am most grateful at this stage in my life that I care more about helping someone avoid the traps and mistakes I made than I do about what people think of me. Your life is a journey and every step you take, good or bad, is woven into the fabric of your existence and becomes a part of what is needed to make you who you were created to be. May this writing somehow aid in giving you the desire and the courage to take that next step.

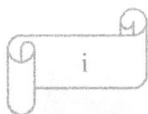

Acknowledgements

My Heavenly Father --- How do I begin? You are magnificent and there are no words that can adequately express how grateful I am for all that You have been to me and all that You have brought me through. Thank You for being true to Your Word and performing it in every area of my life. Thank You for giving me everything I needed to overcome the obstacles, trials and tribulations so that I could make it to this place in my life. Thank You for the gifts and abilities that You've placed within me and for the courage I now have to use them to the fullest. I know I never have to walk alone and that brings me such great comfort. Please use this writing as a tool to bless those who read it and allow it to somehow grant them the courage to do the inner work that is necessary to bring freedom to their souls. I love You more than words can say!

Markisha Barber --- You are one of God's greatest gifts to me and my inspiration to follow the path of truth, knowing that it leads to abundant blessings. May you not follow in my footsteps but rather seek something higher and greater so you don't make the same mistakes I did. If you keep God first, you are destined for greatness and I anxiously await the birthing of all that God has placed inside of you. I love you with all my heart and I'm so proud to be your Mom.

Annette Johnson --- I love you like a daughter. You are intelligent and beautiful and you will make a profound impact upon this world. Always do what you know is right. I continue to expect great things.

Christine Anderson-Payne --- My sister, my friend. May we continue to grow closer as the days go by. Thank you for the early years. I can only imagine all that it took to do what was required. I

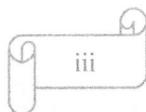

know it was a great sacrifice and I appreciate all that you did to accomplish the task.

Jasmine Anderson --- You are the family's miracle child and your purpose is divine.

Michael, Tinisha and Micah Carroll and Nicholas Payne --- You've defeated the odds and you remain strong in your commitment to one another. May God continue to bless you as a family unit. Your love for each other inspires me.

Christopher and Arkavion Smith; Ashley Thomas --- Chris, God has a magnificent purpose for your life. You may not understand what that means right now, but as the years continue to pass, God will reveal all the answers. Just ask Him. Ashley, thank you for the latest family addition, sweet little Arkavion.

Mark, Evonne, Milah and Mijah Smith --- Your marriage is an example of tenacity and strength. I know it is not always easy to maintain a strong connection with the one you love, but you two give me hope that it can be done; a beautiful family indeed.

Apostle Gerald Grandison, Sr. --- Since the first day I walked into your church until now, you have been there for me, whether in person or in spirit. You have walked me through every trial and celebrated every triumph over the last 26 years. Thank you for being my spiritual father and for taking on the task of dealing with me through the good and the bad. Only God knows just how much you mean to me. Thank you for all your love and support.

Minister Katrina Harling --- It seems like a lifetime. After more than 20 years, it feels like one, too. You have held up my hands when all seemed lost. I don't know how to even begin to thank you for all you've done and those two words just aren't enough. You are an invaluable part of my life and I appreciate you tremendously.

LaShan Haynes --- Oh, how God has used you to bless me. I don't have enough space or time to give you the applause that you deserve. Just know that your dedication to me and my ministry has been a priceless treasure. I love you, my dear sister in Christ.

Bernice Little-Mundle and Inithia Cooper --- The two of you entered my life so many years ago; in elementary school, during the playground phase and we have grown up together. We are lifetime friends and this means so much to me in a world where genuine people are hard to find. Thank you both for your love and support all these years.

There are many others who have spoken into my life along the way, all of whom I love and appreciate very much. I would like to thank all those whose pastoral leadership helped me become the person I am today. I would like to give special thanks and appreciation to Minister Maria Wright and Minister Selwyn Cox. You are angels in disguise. Thank you for allowing God to use you to bless me.

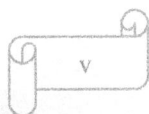

Table of Contents

Introduction - Know Why

My reason for writing this is to convey to women who have been broken and wounded that you are not alone. We have a way of isolating ourselves when we go through painful situations and experiences because we feel a sense of shame and embarrassment. It is during those times that we must embrace the fact that we are deeply loved, forgiven and cared for by our Heavenly Father. His Word tells us there is no condemnation to those who are in Christ Jesus, who do not walk according to the flesh, but according to the Spirit (Romans 8:1).

If you are feeling rejected, ashamed, alone, unworthy or misunderstood, I wrote this book for you. I wrote it to give you the courage to stand up and speak up for yourself. I wrote it to attempt to pass along to you the feelings of self-love and worthiness that come along with a closer walk with God. Once you begin to understand how much HE loves and wants you, you will become much less dependent on people for that love. You will lose the desire to receive man's approval and you will become empowered to live the life God intended when He created you.

For every decision you make in life, know why. That way, no matter what happens, you will always be able to explain to yourself and to God the reasons for your actions. Never do things that don't feel right inside. Your conscience is there for a reason. Allow it to be your guide. In an act of obedience, submit your will to God in exchange for His will for your life. It's a decision you will never regret.

In His Love,
Lisa

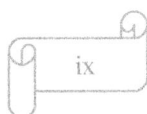

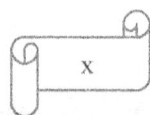

Chapter 1 - Forgotten

Lesson: You must know your identity in Christ. Your Heavenly Father will never leave you behind.

I was born the youngest of four girls and there was a significant age difference between my sisters and myself. They were born one year apart and were 9, 10 and 11 years old when I was born. My mother was a Nurse's Assistant and worked a variety of shifts at a local hospital. When her shift at work kept her from picking me up from school, the task fell to one of my sisters or another family member.

One of my earliest childhood memories was a devastating one. I was five years old in the Kindergarten. One particular afternoon, I waited on the playground to be picked up and no one came. I was left on the playground alone after school. I should have been picked up by a sibling that day but it seems they forgot me. It is easy to see how this could happen. When you are 14, 15 and 16 years old, the last thing on your mind is picking up your little sister from school. Teenagers should not be given parental tasks but it happens quite often if there is a shortfall within the family unit. This incident would follow me throughout the rest of my life and ultimately set the tone of how I operated on a daily basis – *trying not to be forgotten.*

Trying not to be forgotten, you over-compensate so as to seem necessary. You do more than you should for as many as you can. This way, you become indispensable; or so you think. This is an attempt to avoid being thrown away. You spend so much time on the needs of others that you ignore the needs of self. If you're ever left without an "assignment", you're befuddled; wondering what you should be doing at that particular moment. You know more about others than you know about yourself. You become a great "need meeter". Burnout is inevitable. It may take years, but it will come. When it happens, it seems like the whole world comes crashing down around you all at once. Each present failure brings back the memory of a failure from the past. You start reliving old offenses and nursing old wounds that should have healed a long time ago. You allow your mind to wander and you eventually lose control of your thoughts. You become very negative. This is a sure sign of attack by the enemy. In order to turn this around, you must allow the peace of God to guard your heart and mind (Philippians 4:7) so as not to fall into an emotional depression.

No one wants to feel like they are not wanted or needed. Rejection is a terrible thing. It's painful. We don't want to experience it but it creeps into the lives of the best of us. The feelings of rejection leave scars as deep as the ocean. Left unchecked, these feelings creep into every empty crack and crevice of your being. You secretly come to expect it from everyone to whom you're connected. That is why it is so important to fill your spirit with as much of God's Word as possible. If the feelings of rejection are not dealt with, they lead to many failed and unhealthy relationships.

You desperately search for acceptance and love. You end up looking for love in all the wrong places. You want so much to be held, shielded and protected from the pain that's already taken root deep down on the inside. You don't even realize that the worst has already happened. You're already sad, already lonely, already hurt, already broken. If you would only pay attention to yourself, you would see that your biggest fears have already manifested but you will discover (to your own amazement) that somehow, you survived. You suddenly gain the strength to ask yourself "what can happen now that hasn't already?"

With the answer to this question comes a deeper understanding of self. You begin to realize that it is time to allow God to turn your tragedy into triumph and that the only way to get through is to actually GO through. Psalm 23 says "yea, though I walk through the valley of the shadow of death"; not as I pull over, not as I park, not even as I stop off, but as I walk through. You have to keep walking, keep trying, keep pushing, keep pressing, keep praying, keep believing, keep trusting and most of all keep going and know that God is walking right along with you.

The closer you get to God, the more you begin to understand that you can never be truly forgotten because of His great love for you. One of our problems is that we seek to draw closer to man than we do to God. This was never God's intention. His Word says "draw nigh to me and I will draw nigh to you" (James 4:8) and "I will never leave nor forsake you" (Hebrews 13:5). It takes a mature, well-developed relationship with God to really understand what that means. If you don't take the time to draw close to God, you will not be able to effectively feel His Presence. It is critical that you are able to do this. The enemy takes great delight in being able to keep you separated from God. The more time you spend in His Word, the more you are able to detect and divert the tactics of the enemy.

Once you discover your identity in Christ, you will begin to understand who you are as an individual. God takes great delight in you and rejoices over you with singing (Zephaniah 3:17), which means you are someone special. You can't understand how to properly love yourself without God's help. God's love for us is beyond human comprehension.

At some point, it's time to decide to adapt God's attitude concerning you. If He can love you enough to send His own Son to die for you, why can't you love yourself? We must not buy into any of the tricks the enemy uses to keep us in conflict with ourselves. Many times, he uses our physical attributes to trip us up. He tells us things like, you're too fat; you're too skinny; you're ugly; you're stupid; you're not good enough. Once we take the bait, it's all downhill from there. We become so consumed with our outer selves that we ignore the inner self --- our spirit man or spirit woman. We need God's Word to strengthen the inner self. There are no over-the-counter drugs for the spirit.

You must ground yourself in a good Bible-believing, Bible-teaching church. It must be a place that ministers to the total you. You must not only learn what the Word says, but you must also learn how to apply it to your life in everyday, practical ways. You must learn how to **live** the Word of God. Once you are able to do this, your life will drastically change. You will be able to experience the peace of God (Philippians 4:7) and the joy of the Lord (Nehemiah 8:10) in ways that you never could before. Your appetite will change (spiritually and naturally). You will begin to attract quality into your life and you will develop a spirit of discernment that will allow you to see and understand things you couldn't see and understand before.

God becomes more real to you. You begin to sense His Presence and to feel His touch. Your prayer life deepens and you begin to crave the things of God. You want more and more of Him and nothing else will do. Your greatest desire is to be obedient and to perform the will of God for your life. You finally learn how to love yourself and then you ultimately realize that what you were searching for on the outside was already residing within. Your unhealthy dependence on human approval fades into the background and you become secure in the person our Heavenly Father created you to be. You find out that if God is all you have, then He really is all you need!

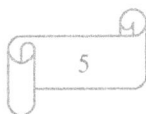

Lisa Gillespie

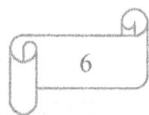

Chapter 2 - Liberated but Lost

Lesson: You must be mature enough to handle freedom. This requires total surrender to God.

When I was 19 years old, I decided it was time to leave the nest. I didn't like the atmosphere that was created by a bunch of grown women trying to live together in the family home, so I decided it was time to be on my own. I searched for an apartment without discussing my plans with my Mom. When I got the keys, I had an extra set made and gave them to her along with the announcement that I was moving out. She wasn't happy. I thought I was doing something that would make her proud; instead, she made me feel like I was deserting her and what was supposed to be a happy time turned sad. She didn't help me move into my new apartment and it took about four months before she even inquired as to where I lived, but in time she finally accepted this change and things began to improve. She even started coming over for visits.

Despite this less than desirable beginning, I was glad to be on my own. I was free. I didn't know that although I was liberated (naturally), I was still lost (spiritually). Being saved is one thing; being born again is another. Salvation means accepting Christ as your Lord and Savior. New birth embraces the change that should come along with that acceptance. I received salvation but I remained carnal (worldly). This is very dangerous. When you are a carnal Christian, you care more about the flesh than the spirit. Your flesh dominates every action and decision and you become emotionally wreckless. The enemy gives you a false sense of security that makes you feel like you can do whatever you want without consequences.

Adolescent independence can be good and bad. On one hand, you think you know it all and on the other hand, you know you don't but you're too proud to own up to needing guidance from those who are wiser and more experienced than you. It was during this time that I started the first round of foolish turns in my life. I started dating a married man. This is NEVER wise. Adultery and fornication violate the laws of God. It is a violation of the marriage covenant.

At this age and stage of my life, there was only one thing I could offer a married man and we all know what that was. Being married, he couldn't legitimately offer me anything but a promise that the marriage was already over (which is usually a lie) and that when his kids were older, he would leave his wife and marry me. Somehow, I managed to convince myself that we were in love and that what he was telling me was true. Being raised without a father left me without the healthy emotional self-esteem that young girls need, so I believed everything this man told me and allowed my morals and values to be compromised, which was a huge mistake.

You see, a part of me was still five years old on the playground waiting to be "picked up". Although I was grown now, I was still waiting to be rescued, loved, held and protected. I did not realize that I already had all these things in God. When you are not close enough to God, you can't benefit from the things that come along with being in His presence. I didn't know God valued me beyond measure, so I was still looking for a man to do that.

I wanted someone to love me so I allowed myself to believe that I found that love in a man who was not mine to have; all the while, trying to convince myself that it was okay because of how it made me feel. I felt cared for, valued and appreciated and I was fooled into believing my needs were being met. I didn't feel rejected anymore because I was with someone who wanted to be with me. At the time, it didn't matter to me that he was forbidden fruit. This was someone who spent time with me, not because he had to, but because he wanted to. I couldn't see that this was a trick of the enemy. Do you see how dangerous deception is? This type of revelation only comes with spiritual maturity and wisdom.

My spiritual constitution was not strong enough for me to see just how wrong this was. I did not realize that I was setting myself up for future disaster by violating the laws of sowing and reaping. You see, you really do reap what you sow, positive or negative; good or bad. Because I was planting seeds of dishonesty now, I would have to reap a harvest of dishonesty later. The enemy never tells you the whole story, just the part that will get you to do the thing he desires so he can accuse you before God. I finally woke up and realized that I was in a dead end relationship that could not offer me what I truly desired and deserved. I ended the relationship and decided to seek something higher for myself.

Shortly afterwards, I met the man I would marry. The idea of marriage was exciting to me but because of the seeds I planted prior to marriage, the harvest that was produced ultimately affected my marriage. My husband was not finished with a relationship he was in prior to meeting me and, unbeknownst to me, continued that relationship during our marriage. Can you see the tangled web? We had other difficulties as well but once I learned the truth, I wasn't willing to attempt to repair the damage because our marriage was not based on truth and the little bit of trust that had been built was now torn down. Of course, I was hurt but I couldn't really be angry because all I was doing was reaping from the harvest I had sown. That's why it is important to think before you act.

Just because you're old enough to live on your own doesn't give you the right to do anything you want to do. Yes, you are allowed to make all of the decisions that concern you but you must be grounded in God's Word in order to be able to make the right decisions. Flesh and spirit will never agree and most of what your flesh tells you to do is against the Word of God. You must be strong enough to say no. Those who are young are not usually equipped with this type of strength.

It is said that "with age comes wisdom"; sometimes yes and sometimes no. Where is it written that you have to be old to be wise? The Bible says if anyone lacks wisdom, let Him ask God (James 1:5). I am attempting to equip my young sisters with wisdom that, at their age, I did not possess. I didn't always listen to the things my mother told me at the time she said them. I want you to have the opportunity to stop and reconsider some things you're about to do before you actually do them. Think about the effects your actions will have, not only on you, but on your children (whether they are born yet or not) and your grandchildren. Certain consequences last a lifetime. Examine what the Bible says in Exodus 20 about sin and future generations. This means that what you're about to do won't affect just you. This is where generational curses originate. Do you really want to start this vicious cycle? Do you know any women who were teenage mothers and then their daughters became teenage mothers? Do you know any parents who were alcoholics and their children became alcoholics? Do you know any parents who were drug addicts whose children became drug addicts? You can't set yourself on fire and not get burned! Whatever you constantly do eventually catches up with you and whatever you constantly live becomes a part of your story.

Yes, I was liberated but I still wasn't free. You can only be free in Christ Jesus. At that time in my life, He was only a small part of the equation. I thought I knew what was best for me and I was very, very wrong because my thoughts were very far from God's thoughts (Isaiah 55:8). He is the One with the master plan and in order to know what that plan is, we must allow Him to be the Master. We must seek His will for our lives rather than attempt to implement our own. This is the only real way to success.

Lisa Gillespie

Chapter 3 - Enlightened

Lesson: You must be willing to face the reality and consequences of your choices. Honesty is key.

When I was 21 years old, I found out that I was fathered by someone other than my mother's husband. I was given the shocking news that the person I was raised to believe was my father was not. My real father, who had always been in my life (but in a different capacity) died and during the week of preparation for his funeral, I was told that he, in fact, was my father. I can't put into words how hard this revelation hit me. He was a well-known person, prominent in his line of work, so I could not share this with anyone without putting his reputation, as well as my mother's, in jeopardy.

There are so many feelings that go along with this kind of revelation. At first, you're angry and you have a lot of questions. Then you start to feel like you are guilty of doing something wrong, even though it's not your fault. A shroud of secrecy looms over your life and you start to wonder if you'll ever be free to reveal who you really are.

Children need what both parents have to offer. The roles of mother and father are very different. Why do we think that it's okay to single-handedly raise children when it takes two people to make a child? Please understand that I am not knocking being a single parent, if it comes to that. I was one myself. What I am saying is that just because I felt I no longer needed my daughter's father as my husband did not mean that she no longer needed him as her father.

A mother cannot be a father; a father cannot be a mother. The child needs the involvement of both parents. This is why we must take the time to get ourselves together before we have children. If girls grow up without their fathers, they experience a void where that father's love should have been and it rarely goes away. This void impacts the way she interacts with boys and ultimately men. Because she has nothing to pattern her choices after, she begins to accept wrong things as right. She doesn't know it's not okay not to be treated like a lady because she is just glad to have a man's attention. She doesn't recognize the qualities of a real man because she's never seen how a real man operates. This leads to many poor relationship choices and bad decisions.

That's why it is necessary to really consider the attributes of the man who will father your children. You have more to consider than just whether he's good in bed. When you decide to have intercourse with a man, you must ask yourself, "if I get pregnant, is this person worthy to father my child?" This is more important than I know how to explain. If he is not worthy, you are not the only one who will have to deal with that. You can later decide not to be bothered with him but your child will not have the luxury of making that choice. Your children will have to deal with him and all his inadequacies for life. If he leaves, they are the ones who will miss his involvement the most. It is too late after a child is born to figure out that his father is still a child himself. Make sure he's a man before you sleep with him. Men, this also applies to you in regards to the women you choose.

I didn't miss out on one father, I missed out on two. I thought to myself "how could this happen?" My mother's husband died when I was just five years old. She and my birth father previously agreed to keep the truth a secret and I was never to know otherwise. But then he died and I guess she just couldn't hold on to it any longer. I was really scarred because I never got over not having a father's love in my life growing up. When I found out that my second chance to have that love was intentionally kept secret from me, I was beyond angry. This is why we must be upfront and honest about the choices we make. It is never right to pass off one man's child as the child of another. If you're having unprotected sex with multiple partners and you get pregnant, how will you know who the father is? One day, the truth will come out. This causes a great deal of pain on many fronts. In the end, the child is the one who suffers the most.

The only way I was able to move beyond the void that was created was to learn to accept the love and care of my Heavenly Father in place of the two earthly fathers who passed on. Now, I believe that this was God's intention all along. He is our Father but we can't experience Him that way with a surface relationship. We must have a deeper connection with Him in order to feel that Father-Daughter bond. God is greater than anyone and anything and the care and nurture He provides will always be more than enough. The way to get to know that is through worship and the Word. You must become a true worshipper so that God can reveal His nature to you.

You must spend one on one quality time with God. You must read, study and meditate on His Word, which will nourish your spirit in ways you cannot imagine. When you reach a certain level in God, you will become more secure about who you are as a person and in who He is as your Father. He makes it clear to you through His Word just how valuable and precious you are to Him. What you thought you missed out on from your earthly Father will be replaced by what you receive from your Heavenly Father. You will discover that no amount of human involvement can compare with what you are receiving from God. The closer you get to God, the closer He gets to you. It was never God's intention for me to dwell on the fact that I grew up without an earthly father in my home. On the contrary, He wanted me to depend on Him to meet my every need.

If you find yourself in this same position, please don't let it take you as long as it took me to realize the golden opportunity that is yours. If your earthly father is not in your life in a productive and fulfilling way, turn to your Heavenly Father. He is everything you are seeking and more. God has so much to give His girls and He loves us beyond measure. He is waiting for us to love ourselves enough to put down the superficial and prepare ourselves to receive the authentic. He wants us to stop living beneath our privileges and begin to desire for ourselves what He desires for us. Give your Heavenly Father a chance to do what His Word promised He would. No one can love you like your Father can.

As long as you live like you don't know who you are, all kinds of unfortunate things will continue to happen to you. God has given us the power to make positive things happen. Why do we sit around and *wait* for something to happen when we have the power to *make* something happen? There is no amount of devastation that can abort your destiny, unless you allow it to do so. Make a firm determination that you will allow God to fill every void in your life until such time as you receive what He intended to occupy that particular space. Don't move ahead of Him but don't lag behind

Him either. Walk *with* God; step by step and day by day. He will teach you as much as you desire to learn. It's never too late to begin again.

Lisa Gillespie

Chapter 4 - Rushed

⚒

Lesson: Never rush into marriage. Sacred things should never be disrespected.

✗

My first marriage (previously mentioned) happened when I was 24 years old. We only dated for about six months. He was in ministry and we allowed outside pressure to cause us to rush into a decision to get married before we took the necessary time to get to know all the things two people need to know about themselves and each other before they take a step of this magnitude. Because of our haste, this marriage only lasted for a little over two years.

Neither of us fully understood what we were getting ourselves into when we got married. As previously stated, I did not know he was not completely finished with some loose ends from his past. Those loose ends coupled with a lack of maturity on both parts cost us our marriage. He was not completely honest about everything and I was not equipped to forgive the way a wife should. Because we were untrained in adversity, when troubled times arose, we could not withstand the storm. We separated when our daughter was nine months old and never reconciled. This is when I remembered the seeds of dishonesty I planted in the years prior to meeting him and now felt as though they were finding their way back to me.

God's Word warns against extra-marital affairs. I would now have to experience the effects of my poor behavior earlier in life. I began to understand the consequences of my improper relationship during this marriage. Because I participated in unfaithfulness prior to my marriage, I had to personally experience unfaithfulness within my marriage. It is critical that we understand that what we put out sooner or later returns to us. Even though I was single while dating a married man, it was still wrong.

Some things should never be rushed. A decision to marry is one of those things. There are SO many things you need to know about a person before you marry them. This goes for men and women. After all, this is the person with whom you are agreeing to spend your life. The vows say "for better or worse" and "till death do us part". This is not lightweight stuff, it's heavy. This is not something you just jump into and if it doesn't work, decide to go your separate ways. Marriage is a covenant, not just a contract. Contracts are more easily broken than covenants. We unfortunately take the world's advice on how to resolve conflict more frequently than God's advice, which is His Word.

We rarely take the time to consider how divorce will affect our children. As women, we get so wrapped up in our pain and that's all we can see at the moment. In time, husbands and wives may get over it, but sometimes the children never do. They spend the rest of their childhood being shuffled back and forth between their parents and if the parents are not able to maintain a cordial relationship, even that becomes increasingly difficult. We can change spouses but the children can't change parents. Your biological parents can never be changed. The children should never feel they have to choose between one or the other, or side with either of you in matters concerning family business.

It's just so sad that while we're going through these problems, we can't see clearly enough to know what's really going on. Most of the time, it takes hind sight to shed some light on what we should have done. Hopefully, it's not too late for someone reading this to make smarter choices than the ones I did. First, take time to get to know who you are and to determine your individual wants and needs. Then, get to know the person you plan to marry, deeply, personally and intimately (and I'm not talking about sex). This process doesn't happen in a few weeks or months. Ignore outside pressure to rush into a marriage. Most of the time, people rush into marriage because of the sex factor. We know we're not supposed to have sex outside of marriage, so we rush into it just to make the sex "legal". Later, we find out all the things we should have known about before we took that step. Unfortunately, a whole lot more time will be spent outside of the bedroom than inside and that's the part where we find the most difficulty.

Since this commitment is forever, it should be entered into at a very slow and deliberate pace. If you see red flags, please do not ignore them; they're there for a reason. Your God-given instincts are there for a reason as well. Pay attention to them. If you feel like something's wrong, most likely it is. You should always investigate, ask questions and communicate. You and your significant other must be able to communicate. How can you consider marrying someone you can't even talk to? Poor communication alone ends many marriages.

Please start now and learn to trust your own instincts. No one knows you better than you and God. If you don't know yourself, you're missing out on some very important information. We must know ourselves so that during moments of crisis, we do not need to ask others what we should do. We know it is more fitting to go to God and get our advice from Him, yet often this is the last thing we do. God will always tell you the truth. He will never lie or sugar-coat the truth. He will not tell you what you want to hear; He'll tell you what you need to hear. He will help you learn how to recognize and hear the voice of His Holy Spirit inside of you. This way, you always remain in control of what happens to you and you rarely become a victim of circumstance.

Resist the urge to rush into major decisions. The enemy loves haste because he knows that when we're rushing, we're usually not thinking clearly. Think back on a few of the mistakes you have made. Didn't you ever ask yourself "what might have happened if only I had waited a little while longer?" You are worth the time is takes to slow down and think things through. Don't let anyone rush you into something you're not sure about. The Bible says there is a time for everything (Ecclesiastes 3). There are many benefits in waiting. For example, when driving, if the light turns yellow, it is an indication that we should prepare to stop. Some drivers treat it as a message to hurry up and get through. This is how a lot of accidents happen. This is true for driving and it's also true for life. Make a small change in your life right now. When you see the next yellow light, rather than punching the gas pedal and speeding through, take the opportunity to stop and look around. Who knows? You might see something you've never seen before as well as afford yourself the reward of avoiding an accident.

Chapter 5 - FAVORED

Lesson: Miracles still happen.

During my first marriage, I was given a miracle. During the fall of 1990, I became ill and needed to go to the emergency room for evaluation. Once there, a number of tests were done, followed by a period of waiting for the doctors to determine the cause of my sickness. When the doctor came into the room, he somewhat playfully asked me what I thought was wrong with me. I told him I didn't know, just that I felt sick. He happily informed me that I wasn't sick, but pregnant. What a wonderful surprise! I left the emergency room that day with some very exciting news I could share with the family just in time for the holidays.

Of course, the enemy was not excited about my news. In fact, he did everything he could to take away the miracle God had given. A few days after I discovered I was expecting my first child, I received a call from a doctor at the hospital where I received emergency care. She explained that she was reviewing some of the tests results from my ER visit. She told me that my sac was empty and that I needed to return to the hospital for a D&C, which is a procedure where the cervix is opened and the contents of the uterus is removed. This procedure is often performed after a miscarriage to stop bleeding and prevent infection. You can imagine how upsetting this news was, especially since I was so excited about the pregnancy.

Not wanting to risk my health and well-being, my husband and I prepared to go to the hospital for the procedure as directed by the doctor. When we arrived, we were walking to the hospital entrance when I heard an audible voice say "don't go in". I turned to my husband and said "why not?" He looked at me as if I was crazy and he said "why not what?" I said to him "you said don't go in. Why not?" He said "I didn't say anything". We continued to move toward the entrance and in a louder, even more audible tone, I heard the voice again say "don't go in". By this time, I was irritated. I snapped at my husband and said "do you think this is a joke?" He looked at me and shook his head, asking what in the world I was talking about. I told him "you keep saying don't go in." He assured me he had said nothing. I told him I distinctly heard a male voice say "don't go in". He said, "if that is what you heard, then let's go home". So we did.

The doctor repeatedly called me, telling me that I was risking my life by not coming in for the D&C. I told her what happened outside and she acted as if I had said nothing. This incident took place during a weekend and I told her I would wait until Monday to get in touch with my own doctor. She was extremely emphatic about the fact that I could die before Monday and I told her I would take my chances. Monday came and I called my doctor, who arranged for me to have a sonogram to find out what was going on. Just before going in for the procedure, I prayed for God's will to be done.

I explained everything that happened at the ER and after. The doctor assigned me to a technician and said "she's one of the best. If there's a baby in there, she'll find it". We smiled at each other and the procedure began. After a few minutes, she called the doctor in to take a look at the monitor. They looked at each other, then turned the screen toward me. The doctor said "do you see that blinking

X?" I said yes. He said "that's your baby's heartbeat!" Tears of joy ran down my face. Had I listened to that doctor from the ER, I would have unknowingly aborted my baby. I firmly believe that this was a trick of the enemy. That doctor used every scare tactic there was to try to lure me back into that hospital. She went so far as to say that I would bleed to death if I didn't have the procedure done.

My faith and trust in God would not allow me to listen to her. God demonstrated Jeremiah 29:11 for me in a very personal way. It was His plan for our daughter to be born into this world and I believe her purpose is great. The enemy took great pains to try to instill fear and doubt into me through this doctor. That's why you have to know God for yourself. I was not afraid and I believed God would not allow me to die while I waited to see my own doctor. See, there's that spirit of haste again. Remember that the enemy loves haste. If I had been in a hurry to follow this doctor's advice, I would have missed out on one of the greatest blessings in my life. God is real. He speaks to us through His Holy Spirit. We must learn how to recognize His voice.

Because God is faithful and true to His Word, a miracle occurred on July 26, 1991. A healthy, beautiful baby girl, Markisha Re'Shawn Barber, was born into the world at Holy Cross Hospital in Silver Spring, Maryland. I'm so glad I listened to God when He said "don't go in".

Lisa Gillespie

Chapter 6 - Crushed

Lesson: Guard your heart and be prepared for the unexpected. Always leave room for God's healing without your substitutes.

When I was 28 years old, I found out my oldest sister needed a kidney transplant. I decided to donate my kidney to her in hopes that this would bring us closer together and that we could finally develop the sisterly relationship we never had before. There were a battery of tests in preparation for the donation, but the day finally arrived. The surgery seemed to go well but after a week, the kidney rejected and my sister died. I was crushed. This was the first time in my life that I can recall being mad at God. I couldn't even pray. I was so settled in to my plan that I had not consulted God about His plan. I gave my sister a kidney so that she could live. When that didn't happen, I thought I had failed her and that God had failed us both. I had to learn to trust God's answer. I couldn't see the blessing that was before me. 1 Corinthians 13:13 says "and now abide faith, hope, love, these three; but the greatest of these is love". Before my sister left this world, she was able to experience my love for her through what I had done. She didn't ask me for a kidney, I offered one to her. She lived with that kidney for a short time after surgery and was able to express her gratitude to me, which was it's own priceless treasure.

When my sister died, I grieved in an unusual way. I allowed my season of grief to cause me to cling to man rather than God in an effort to ease my pain. This is always a mistake. It was during this time that I entered into my second marriage, which lasted for a brief nine months. This marriage produced a blended family because the man I married had a son. Because I was still in a season of grief, I was not prepared to handle all that came along with taking on a husband and another child. I was not ready to take on something of this magnitude and I ignored all the warning signs. What I really wanted above all else was to have my sister back. Because that was not possible, I did the next best thing. The man I married and my brother in law were best friends. Because of this, he spent a lot of time around my sister during prior years and knew things about her that I did not know. When she died, she was all he and I talked about. I didn't realize that her memory actually became the basis of our relationship. We would spend hours and hours talking about her and reliving moments from the past. We were building on the wrong foundation.

As I think about it now, this marriage never had a chance to survive because it was based on the wrong things and happened at the wrong time. We may have had sufficient dating time but while we were dating, we did not delve into the things that we needed to examine prior to entering into the marriage relationship. My sister died in June; we married a few months later. I had not yet begun to acknowledge my grief, much less develop a plan to deal with it. I had to heal physically as well as emotionally. The kidney transplant was major surgery. Not only had I lost an organ, I also lost my sister. Having to deal with that alone would have been enough. Rather than deal with these issues head on, I suppressed them and tried to continue on with life as if nothing happened. This was another mistake. If you find yourself in a similar situation, don't do what I did. Deal with the issues in your life as they arise. Don't ignore them and create new ones.

Along with the pressures of being a wife, came the pressures of having two children rather than just one. The children were toddlers, nine months apart and so the motherhood role was much more demanding. I didn't have enough positive emotional energy for myself, much less to handle a husband and two small children. Because I was in denial, I was not able to clearly see what was going on.

When our marriage hit a rocky place, we did not have a strong enough foundation to withstand the turmoil. When you build on sand, all that is needed to blow it away is a strong wind. Joy and sorrow do not go together and you cannot mix the two. I was grieving. How could I ignore that? Grief must be dealt with or it will never go away. If it is suppressed and ignored, it will come out in uglier ways. You must experience the many facets of it and go through the entire process. If you don't, you are headed for disaster and doomed to make decisions that will come back to haunt you later. My unwillingness to acknowledge my grief caused me to make a decision that would affect four lives, not just one. It is always wise to count the cost (Luke 14:28). As the wise builder says, measure twice, cut once. If you don't, you will end up paying more than you want or need to spend.

From this experience, I learned that it is never okay to pretend you are fine when, deep down inside, you know you are not. Don't ignore what is blatantly obvious. Learning to be true to yourself can be painful but also rewarding. You owe it yourself to acknowledge and deal with all the feelings that come your way, good and bad.

Take the time to find out why you are feeling a particular way instead of trying to ignore or dismiss it. Everything happens for a reason.

Chapter 7 - LICENSED

Lesson: Your poor decisions will not change God's mind about who you're destined to become. Answer the call; God's plan will prevail.

There came a time when I began to question the point of my existence. Even though I was still young, I could look back and see all the mistakes I'd made and wonder why I was even here. This is when God started to deal with me concerning my call to preach the gospel. Initially, I was stunned because I felt there was no way God would (or even could for that matter) use someone who was as tainted as I was. I decided to stay as far away from this new revelation as I possibly could and not share it with anyone. God had other plans.

I knew God was calling me and I decided not to answer. I had several warnings before I actually yielded to His call. God told someone very close to me about my calling. When she tried to discuss it with me, I got angry with her. I began to experience frequent illnesses, which culminated with a bit of devastating news. I was having tests done to try to find out what was wrong with me and received a diagnosis of stage four cervical cancer. You can imagine the feelings of desperation that washed over me. My daughter was only two years old at the time and I could not imagine not being able to raise her. At first, I panicked and everything inside of me was screaming for help. Then, I realized what was really going on.

I knew it was time to make a decision. At this point, I would literally live or die and everything else depended on my next move. I informed my Mom and my Pastor of my diagnosis and instructed them not to tell anyone else. I fasted and prayed, believing God would divinely heal me – AND HE DID! There was so much going through my mind at this stage. I knew God had healed me and I also knew why; so that I could fulfill His call on my life. I knew God wanted to use me in this way because of how He was dealing with me in visions and dreams. At first, I was afraid, but the more God shared with me, the more I learned to trust His will for me.

My Pastor scheduled a conference with me to discuss what I had been told by God. At that time, I did not want to acknowledge the truth of my calling because of fear. It is dangerous to know your purpose and blatantly refuse God's direction. Women preachers were not widely accepted and I wasn't ready to join the fight, yet I knew that saying no was disappointing God. I was afraid of what people would say and what they would think. I had to realize who and whose I was. I was not here for man's purposes but for God's. After the conversation with my Pastor and a lot of prayer, I yielded to the call and was licensed to the gospel ministry late in 1993.

There was a lot going on in my life at this point. My sister died five months earlier in June and I got married just a few weeks prior to the licensing. I was trying to juggle being a wife, a working mother of two and a newly licensed minister without having the proper tools that were necessary for success. I had to allow myself to absorb all that God was trying to give and all that He wanted to do with me.

I have always had an awareness of God but awareness is not enough. We must develop a deeply rooted personal relationship with Him in order for our lives to be what He designed them to be. Deep roots take time to grow. You can't plant a seed one day and expect a full grown tree the next. Even though I was preaching God's Word to other people, there were still many voids in my own life that I did not know how to fill. I didn't realize the voids were not mine to fill, they were God's. Before you can minister to others, you must allow God to minister to you. Learn to take care of your own needs first. My ministry could not blossom and truly prosper because I wasn't taking good care of me.

When you have a shallow relationship with God, you are prone to making stupid mistakes. Carnality enables you to be saved but still live like the world. It is imperative that you sell out to God, completely. It will not work if you're half in and half out. Accepting the call involves a willingness to surrender. The psalmist wrote "I Surrender All" and that is exactly what it takes to have an effective connection to God. You cannot effectively grow if you are improperly connected to the Vine. Improper connection causes death; maybe not to the whole tree, but most certainly to the part that is not receiving the proper nourishment.

Lisa Gillespie

Chapter 8 - Raped

⚶

---

*Lesson: **Always report it and
never allow the guilt to hold you
hostage.***

🐦

It was the holiday season and I decided to purchase holiday pictures of my daughter. I used a local, well-known vendor for this task. The day came for us to visit the studio to have the pictures done. When the pictures were taken and processed, I got a call to say they were ready for pickup. When I got to the studio, the photographer told me to give him a minute to find my order. After a few minutes passed, he returned to the counter to tell me that he couldn't find my order with the other orders in the back. He told me that he had other recently processed orders at his house and that he may have accidentally left my order with the others.

I knew this person from high school. I did not know he owned this particular business but once I went in to have the work done and discovered he was in charge, I was surprised to be able to reconnect and catch up on old times. He talked to me about his wife and kids and seemed to have a settled, happy life. When I went to the studio for pickup, I had my Mom and daughter in the car and when he said he had to go to his house to look for the photo order, I offered him a ride with us. When we got to his house, as he got out of the car,

Lisa Gillespie

he asked me to come inside with him. Because he wasn't a total stranger, I didn't think twice about it. This was the wrong move.

When we got inside, he showed me around the main level and then said his in-home studio was upstairs. He told me to follow him. When I got to the third or fourth step, something triggered within my consciousness. I stopped on the stairwell and told him I would wait downstairs. It was already too late. He grabbed my arm and forced me up a few more stairs. I pulled back but could not get away from him. I asked him what he was doing and he said "I think you know". When I realized what was happening, I tried to talk my way out of it by reminding him that my mother and daughter were in the car. He didn't care. He raped me on the stairs inside his home. When it was over, he told me that if I told anyone, he would harm my child.

After the rape, I was too shocked to move. I sat on the stairs, dumbfounded. What had just happened? How did I let myself get into this situation? Why did I even go into the house with him? As I sat on the stairs trying to wrap my mind around all of this, he went upstairs and retrieved my photo order. On the way back down, he looked at me as if nothing happened and said "ok, I got the pictures. Let's go". What? Did he know what he had just done? He acted like nothing happened. When we got back to the car, my mother could tell something was wrong. She asked me but I told her it was nothing. When we dropped him off at the shop, I took my Mom and daughter back to my Mom's house and asked if my daughter could spend the night. When I got home, I cried, took a long, hot bath and called my best friend. I told her what happened.

She told me to immediately report this to the police but I was too afraid because of his threat. I never told anyone this happened because I was so ashamed. I thought it was my fault for going into his house and blamed myself for not being smart enough to avoid this trap. It took me years to stop believing this lie. I was not walking in truth. Rape is never the victim's fault. It is the fault of the perpetrator alone. When a person is violated sexually, the experience is devastating. This is not something anyone should try to go through alone. It takes a certain kind of support to successfully work through this kind of trauma.

I made a big mistake. Bigger than the mistake of going into his house in the first place, was the decision not to report the rape to the police. How many times before had he already gotten away with this, and how many more times in the future? It was obvious that this was not the first time he had done this and I suppose deep down inside, I knew it would not be the last. Yet, I was not grounded enough in God to be willing to take the chance and tell. All I could think about was his threat against my child. Had I known then, what I know now, I would not only have reported the incident to the police but also told as many people as I could so that they would stop patronizing his business. Fear paralyzes you and causes you to make poor decisions. God has not given us a spirit of fear (2 Timothy 1:7), so when fear comes upon us, we know it wasn't God who put it there. We need to stand on the Word and do what we know is right.

I was fortunate enough to have a good support system during the time that I dealt with this tragedy. It took me a long time to stop blaming myself for what happened, but eventually, through counseling, prayer and positive affirmation, I overcame the guilt associated with the incident. I learned how to stop blaming myself and I asked God to help me forgive the offender for violating me this way. I continued to worry that this would happen to others, so I prayed that God would stop this individual from attacking innocent, unsuspecting women.

Remember the laws of sowing and reaping? The Bible says that you reap what you sow (Galatians 6:7). Now I know just how true that is. The rapist who posed as a legitimate business man did strike again and was caught and imprisoned for his crimes. I was sorry that another victim had to suffer through this type of ordeal, but relieved and grateful that this nightmare was finally over. I prayed for peace for myself and for the other victims who suffered at the hands of this vicious criminal.

If you are raped, tell. Tell close friends and family members so they can help you through this difficult time. Tell the police. Rape is a crime, report it. Don't continue to allow your attacker to secretly live within your mind as you relive the details of this horrible crime day after day. Talk about your fears with people you trust. Do what is necessary to guarantee your safety and that of those you love. I did not have the wisdom or the courage to do so when it happened to me and because of it, others had to suffer. Don't ever let something this tragic and devastating happen to you and then try to keep it a secret. Always tell. Do not allow the enemy to trick you into silence. I am not proud that I did not tell back then but I am proud that I have the inner strength to tell now. I strongly believe that my story will help someone gain the courage to handle this situation differently than I did.

Chapter 9 - Displaced & Desperate

Lesson: Don't pretend you can swim if you know you can't; you WILL drown!

Displaced

When I was 33 years old, I was uprooted from my church family. I had attended this particular church for quite some time and was very involved in it's ministry and activities. I allowed false expectations to rob me of a peaceful and protective relationship between myself and my Pastor. We experienced a breach in our relationship because of my inability to distinguish between what was within my right to know and what was not. When you get too close to the spiritual leaders in your life, you begin to believe you have earned the right to know things that really are none of your business. There are those who believe that they should know every detail of their Pastor's life, spiritual and otherwise. This is not the case. We must keep in mind the purpose of a Pastor, which is to lead, but we must also keep in mind that he or she is made of the same thing we are: flesh and blood. I am not making excuses for spiritual leaders to live their lives in a sinful way. The point I'm trying to make is that all humans err and even in spiritual matters, there is a thin line between professional and personal, but the line does exist.

When I left the church, I fell into a trap, that had I stayed, I could have avoided. Everyone needs to feel like they belong. I left the comfort of my spiritual safety net, which created a void within me. When you are displaced, you begin to experience feelings of uncertainty and doubt and it's easy to allow desperation to settle in. You are no longer selective about what you allow into your life because you just want something to hold on to, even if what you're holding doesn't really belong to you. Loss is a hard thing to handle. When you lose something that was important to you, if you're not careful, you will try to replace whatever you lost with whatever is available. This is not good on any level; actually, it's dangerous.

During this time, I met and started dating another married man. There goes that tangled web again. Unlike the first one, this one was actually in the process of divorce proceedings, but that still didn't make it right. He was in transition and needed a place to stay. Never before had I lived with a man who was not my husband, yet I again allowed my morals to be compromised. Here I was, preaching the gospel and at the same time, in a relationship with a man who was not legally free. What a mess! This proves that God did not have my whole heart. This is a very dangerous way to live. When you live like this, you put yourself in a position to become fair game for the enemy and all kinds of ungodly things begin to happen in your life. Once again, I allowed myself to believe that what I was doing was right.

I thought this relationship would eventually lead to marriage. After his divorce, we continued to date and I thought we were on the same page. I did not know that, for this man, I was a means to an end. He was not a "one-woman man". Another woman called me one day to inform me of their relationship. Unfortunately, it took me too long to find out exactly what I was dealing with and I had already invested more time and emotional energy than I should have. Lies were being told and I was confused by the behavior that was being displayed. I finally did what I should have done in the first place. I prayed. The more I cried out to God, the more information I was given. God revealed every lie that was told to me during this relationship and the reasons for those lies. I am grateful that He did not allow me to continue down a dead-end street but gave me the strength and courage to finally confront this man as well as take responsibility for my poor choices. When it was all said and done, I was rewarded with the truth, which fueled my desire to get back on the road God intended.

Desperate

It was February 5, 1998. I went to bed a little after 10 pm. Around 11:30, my telephone rang. When I answered, it was my sister's voice on the other end of the line. She was crying hysterically and I knew something was terribly wrong. I'll never forget her next words – "Janice is dead." Out of shock and disbelief, I asked "Janice who?" She repeated herself. Janice was our sister. My hands were shaking and my heart started to race. The only thing I could think to do was to tell her I was on my way and hang up the phone.

I called a friend, whose reaction was the same as mine – "Janice who?" She agreed to ride with me to my mother's house, so I picked her up and we were on our way. When we arrived, I saw my mother sitting in a chair at the dining room table with the blankest stare I have ever seen on a human face. I thought she might be in shock. Once I started talking to her, I discovered that she was not in shock, just very confused and hurt over what had occurred.

Earlier in the evening, my sister told my mother she had a headache. She took two pain pills and laid down on the sofa to rest. A few hours later when my niece was about to retire to bed, she tried to wake Janice and couldn't. That is when it was discovered that she was dead. No sign, no symptoms. Once I arrived at the house, it was evident that she had been dead for hours and no one in the house knew. They thought she was just asleep. Wow! Can you imagine what that feels like? My sister left behind a toddler, almost two years old. This was yet another blow to us as a family since my oldest sister's death was just five years earlier. My mother was about to bury her second child. From a mother's perspective, this isn't supposed to happen. The parent is supposed to die before the child, right?

My way of coping with this second family tragedy was again to suppress my own grief in an effort to help my mother deal with hers. This is not wise. I guess it was my excuse not to allow myself the time or opportunity to grieve the loss of my sibling. Stop trying to be all things to all people and take time to pay attention to your own needs. My suppression of my own grief in no way aided my mother in dealing with the loss of her daughter and it did me no good at all. It was hard for me to watch my mother go through this level of sadness and not be able to do anything about it. All I could do was pray but in the end, I discovered that was all I needed to do. God is equipped to handle all of life's pressures, trials and disappointments. We just need to surrender to His will and operate within our circle of control.

After the loss of two sisters, I thought we were finished dealing with grief for a while. I was wrong. Just seven months after the loss of my second sister, my mother died. I guess the grief was just too much. This time, I was in shock. I couldn't believe this was happening again and so soon after burying my sister. It all seemed so unreal. This event took me to depths of grief that I never imagined possible. My spiritual life and my relationship with my mother were my stabilizers. Once these two areas were out of order, it seemed like everything else followed suit. Do you see the set-up? The enemy was trying to take me out and I was helping him. By the way I was living my life, what else could I expect? My foundation should have been built on my knowledge of and love for God but that was not the case. I was attending church on a regular basis, but church attendance alone does not mature you in the things of God. Obedience must be your utmost desire. I was still seeking my own way, so my commitment to God wavered.

My mother was my very best friend. She understood me inside and out and I knew she loved me unconditionally. I could talk to her about everything and even when what I needed was correction, she bathed it in love. My mother had been sick for a long time but she kept it from me. I had no idea she was sick and when I found out, her health was rapidly declining. I prayed for God to give me the time I needed to adjust to this devastating news. God answered that prayer and gave me several months to spend with my mother, during which we were able to say all that needed to be said in preparation for her departure.

When she died, I did not allow myself to grieve the way someone who's lost their mother should. Once again, I put on a stiff upper lip and did what was necessary to help with her final arrangements. I even sang a solo at her funeral. Everyone who knew how close we were went to a friend of mine asking her, "what's wrong with Lisa?" They knew what they were seeing wasn't normal and became concerned about my well-being. All the while, I played the game as well as I could. Little by little, my life was unraveling and I had no idea what to do about it. So, I did what we all do. I ignored the warning signs. I fell into a depression and suffered in silence. I publicly pretended everything was okay and privately continued to fall apart.

One spring day, the sun seemed to shine brighter than normal following an afternoon shower. I kept noticing how beautiful the sky became and it caught my attention. I asked God out loud "what does this mean"? His answer was the beginning of a fresh start for me. God let me know that He was dealing with the problems in my life just as He had done to the clouds after the rain – moving them away. I started to pray more and more and became reacquainted with my Lord and Savior, with a deeper love for Him than I was able to feel before.

The more focused and grounded I became, the more I knew it was time to seek some outside help. I went to counseling and received wise instruction from one of God's angels in disguise. Never be afraid to seek out professional help with a therapist or psychiatrist. These people are trained and equipped to deal with human behavior and they understand, and are able to explain, the reasons we do some of the things we do. Without that counseling, I am not sure I would have been able to come through this crisis as quickly as I did. I am grateful to God and the doctor that he used to bring me out of darkness, back into His marvelous light.

Today, I am not displaced or desperate. I have found my place in God. He has given me the strength, the inner courage and the motivation to open my heart to others and to share my story so that someone who is going through the same thing I was can benefit from my pain. Never suffer in silence because you don't have to. There are too many resources available for us not to take advantage of them.

Chapter 10 - ORDAINED

Lesson: You can't make enough mistakes to revoke your destiny. "For I know the plans I have for you says the Lord. Plans to prosper you and not to harm you; plans to give you hope and a future." – Jeremiah 29:11

W hen I was 38 years old, I was ordained to the full work of the gospel ministry. God used my daughter to forewarn me that it was time to work toward the next milestone in my life. One Sunday afternoon, as we were driving home from church, my daughter told me that our Pastor was going to approach me about starting the process for ordination. What she said took me by surprise. She was 12 years old at the time. How could she have known this? This was not the first time God used my daughter to tell me things, so I knew it was something I should consider. Despite the fact that this new revelation made me nervous, I decided I should just pray and ask God to prepare me for what was to come. Several months later, I was indeed approached by the Pastor to begin the ordination process.

Being formally set apart to do God's work was one of the highlights of my life. Like life, ordination was a process; a process that took a great amount of focus and concentration, and there were lessons at every turn. Strict discipline was required and there were many moments when feelings of unworthiness, fear and anxiety crept in. At times, I was afraid I wasn't good enough and that I was going to fail. But after the process was over, I could look back and see all the good that had come as a result of it. It caused me to do a lot of soul searching, self-assessing and inner reflection. It brought the "true me" to the surface.

During this time, I spent a lot of one on one time with God. I learned a great deal more about Him and felt closer to Him as the process came to a close. Man could not help me with the vast array of feelings I was experiencing so I had to rely solely on God. As always, God came through for me in ways that exceeded my expectations. Not only was I being prepared for ordination, I was learning who I really am. There were revelations about God as well as revelations about self.

The ordination process showed me just how important it is to study the Word of God for yourself. As I prepared myself, I learned in a very deep and meaningful way just how much God loves me. I learned how committed God is to me. I also learned that He has gone to great lengths to secure my freedom through His Son. If I had known this so many years earlier, I would not have made all the foolish decisions I made and taken all those wrong turns. My spiritual constitution would have been stronger and I would have known how to say no to things I should have stayed away from.

You don't have to be in the process of ordination to develop a deeper relationship with God. You just need to surrender your will for His, study and live His Word and worship Him for who He is. Stop complaining about the problems in your life and instead begin to search out the lessons and opportunities for growth that lie before you. Don't try to rush through the process of developing a closer walk with God. Participate in and grow through every phase of the process without attempting to skip any steps. Follow the path God lays out for you, even when you don't fully understand why He is leading you in that particular direction. Surrender total control to Him and rest on His promises. Then, you will be rewarded with a tree that bears much fruit.

Lisa Gillespie

Chapter 11 – Persistent

Lesson: The timing of marriage should be decided by both partners. If either party hesitates, it's not the right time.

When I was 43 years old, I entered into my third marriage. After two failed marriages, I was hesitant at first to even entertain the idea but always knew that I did not want to live my life alone. Because of the way I was raised, I knew that I wanted to have someone to share day to day life with as well as someone with whom I could give and receive love. God's Word says "it is not good for man to be alone" (Genesis 2:18) and I wholeheartedly agree.

It all started off very innocently. I was friends with my intended prior to anything romantic or intimate. He was in the middle of a crisis and turned to me for support. It was a very difficult time and there were a lot of tears and prayers. After his crisis was over, he made me aware of his interest in beginning a relationship with me. We agreed to give it a try. We dated for a number of years and the courtship experience went very well. Finally, I felt it was time to make a decision about the future. At this point, the thought of marriage did not appeal to him so the relationship ended. After a brief period, he changed his mind and asked me to marry him. I thought he was ready, so I said yes.

Somewhere between courtship and marriage, something went wrong. As the wedding day approached, it seemed as if we were on different pages, but we did not agree on this point, so things continued on as planned. We began our marriage on somewhat shaky ground. Something inside kept telling me that something was wrong. Just prior to the wedding, I asked if there was any reason why we should not do it. No reason was given, so amidst doubt and hesitation, the marriage took place. This should NEVER happen. Never marry someone who hesitates; not even a little. Hesitation is a red flag that should not be ignored. You'll be more fulfilled with someone when marriage is what they really want. If your commitment level is unequal, this will come back to haunt you.

When your gut tells you something, listen. I knew something wasn't right but because I was so excited about having someone to share my life with and no longer having to live alone, I allowed the voice of truth to be silenced by fantasy. I ignored the warning signs and pressed forward into a decision that would ultimately prove unwise. It is never wise to settle. Wait for the right person – the one who has the same spiritual values and goals as you do. Wait for the right time – a time that both parties feel is right. Don't compromise on things you know are critical to your personal success and well-being. When you know something's wrong, speak up and get things out in the open. Resist the urge to emotionally withdraw. You have a right to express your thoughts and feelings, even when the truth hurts.

Never lose yourself just to have a mate (this goes for men and women). God made you who you are for a reason. You will never be successful at being someone you weren't created to be. God made you once and He did it right the first time. Wait for the person who is compatible with who God created you to be. If you have to force the issue, then he or she is not the one. True love is pure and it's not hard to maintain. It's when we try to fit a square peg into a round hole that the problems surface. You don't have to beg someone to be with you; just wait for the one God made for you.

Lisa Gillespie

Chapter 12 - Broken

Lesson: Deal with past issues before they become part of your present; then forgive.

A few months into the marriage, the holes in our relationship began to show. I was never convinced that there was a total commitment to the marriage. During our first explosive argument, extremely harsh words were said and I was completely caught off guard. I was devastated. So much so, that I left the family home for several months. When doubt is present from the start, as soon as something bad happens, it is easy to react rather than respond. Our ability to communicate and work through situations was tested and we failed.

During the separation period, I began counseling in an effort to understand how I ended up in this position again. Counseling helped me process what was happening and made me open to communicating about what was going on. After several meetings and in-depth conversations, we decided to give it another try. Even when you're hurting, it is not wise to give in to the temptation to cut off communication with your spouse. This is what the enemy wants. As long as the level of communication remains respectful, always remain open.

Lisa Gillespie

When I moved back into the family home, I returned with all the hopes and dreams that a fresh start can bring. Things seemed to go well for a few months, then would spiral downward all over again. I began to understand more about the reasons why the problems were occurring whereas before, I was only able to see the problems themselves. From time to time, harsh words continued to be spoken. It seemed like we were right back where we started. Do you see how old patterns that are not dealt with surface over and over again? This is where unresolved issues began to arise. I was reliving the poor treatment I had received in years past and it looked very much like what was happening now. I tried over and over to clearly express how I felt but nothing worked. I felt lied to and abused and I was very deeply scarred. I discovered that we did not understand each other and what I thought were commonalities turned out to be vast differences. We had a lot of learning to do, about ourselves and each other.

As the problems continued, I was accused of "running" every time something went wrong. I was told that "running" doesn't solve problems. I could not get my message across; that ignoring problems doesn't solve them either. It seemed like more talking equaled less listening. Nothing was being done about the problems and yet I was expected to remain. I felt like I was out of options and in desperate search of hope.

It appeared that neither of us ever learned to completely forgive and forget. We were secretly nursing old wounds and taking out frustrations on each other. Our slates were not clean, so we could not give each other the benefit of the doubt. I was trying to do everything I knew to make things better, yet nothing worked. This is when I turned to God more and more because I had no place else to go. I discovered that I needed to give God more of me. I knew He deserves nothing less. It took all this turmoil that was going on for me to realize that God had a large piece of my heart, just not the whole thing. This is a mistake women often make in relationships. The Bible tells us to "keep your heart with all diligence, for out of it spring the issues of life" (Proverbs 4:23). I believe that means we should guard our hearts and operate on a daily basis from a strong connection with God as our source, not with man as our source. Very often, we allow people to function as "little gods" in our lives and we give more time and attention to their wants and needs instead of staying focused on what God is directing us to do. You cannot effectively serve God with a divided heart. Once you give God your whole heart, your spiritual vision will become crystal clear. Things you once pondered and wondered about will be revealed to you. Questions you have asked will be answered and confusion will dissipate. You will begin to know and be able to sense the presence of God and you will no longer need to ask others what you should do. You will have the confidence to go to God in prayer and you will know when He has answered.

Several promises were made while attempting to save the marriage. In the end, the promises were not kept. Assigning blame is not important because when relationships fail, both parties are at fault in some way. What is important is that as individuals, we remain true to ourselves. We must show those close to us who we really are and give them the opportunity to decide whether they can handle it or not. Give those you say you love the benefit of knowing the "real you". Don't keep silent and pretend things are alright when you know deep down inside that they are not. I finally realized I was fighting a losing battle because I was fighting alone. It seemed as if this was a lost cause; not because God isn't able, but because nothing changed. God has given us free will but if we don't use that free will to obey what He tells us to do, our lives will be full of all kinds of trials and tribulations.

Lisa Gillespie

Be careful who you choose to love. Be careful who you tell your secrets to. Be careful to whom you open the door of your heart. Never ignore that inner nudge that tells you when something isn't right. There's an old phrase that says "follow your heart". I want to add something to that. It's okay to follow your heart, just don't leave your head completely out of the equation! Allow the two to link up together – your heart AND your head. If one or the other doesn't agree, take the time to find out why. You don't have to rush your way through life making poor decisions. Slow down long enough to figure out what you really want for yourself before you start involving others. If you are unfulfilled within, then it's not a good time to begin a serious relationship.

Chapter 13 - AWAKE

Lesson: Learn to trust the inner voice inside. It is always right.

I am no longer living on fantasy island. I have learned how to see things as they really are. I am able to accept what God allows, even if it's not what I originally wanted. I wake up each day with a joy inside my heart that I am unable to explain. I know this is nothing but the grace of Almighty God. I no longer live in regret over things that have happened in my past. I have been able to make peace with what was and use the lessons learned to create what is to come. I am able to *feel* God's love and care for me and it is better than any other feeling I have ever experienced. Because I have accepted God's forgiveness for all that I have done, I am now able to extend forgiveness to those who need it from me. I have escaped the trap of bitterness that the enemy set for me. It was his desire to isolate me, in an effort to take my life. The feelings of loneliness I used to experience are no longer a part of my daily existence. God's Word says He will never leave or forsake us and once you learn to experience this promise, loneliness becomes a thing of the past.

I still want love in my life but I am no longer desperately in pursuit of it at any cost. I am equipped to patiently wait for the one God will send to fulfill this desire within me, but only if that is His will.

I know that if God is preparing him, then He is also preparing me. There is nothing more beautiful than the joining of two hearts that are completely whole in God. The level of expectation is different when you are connected to someone who is also connected to God. Both of you are leaning and depending on God to meet your needs, rather than each other. The Presence of God takes the pressure off both people to meet unrealistic expectations. When you are whole in God, you are not looking for someone to complete you because you understand that God already has. You are free to become an asset to someone's life rather than a liability.

I no longer look for love in all the wrong places. As a matter of fact, I'm not "looking" for love at all. I am content to wait, believing that love is looking for me. The Word says "he who finds a wife, finds a good thing", not she who finds a husband. If it is within God's plan, He will allow me to be found. If you find yourself in this situation and you're impatient in the area of relationships, here are a few things you can do while you wait. Make a list of the qualities and attributes you want in a husband and I am not talking about tall, dark and handsome (although that wouldn't hurt!). I am speaking more along the lines of spiritual qualities and attributes rather than physical. Pray for him and his relationship with God. Apply your faith to the situation and believe that God will answer your prayer. Also, pray for yourself. Pray that God's keeping power will sustain you while you wait so that you don't fall into any of the traps the enemy sets. Most of all, before you entertain the idea of settling into a new relationship, make sure you know who you are and what you want for yourself and decide not to settle for anything less.

Chapter 14 - VICTORIOUS

Lesson: Rewards await you when you come to the end of yourself. God has already mapped out your success.

I am living proof that no matter what you go through in life, you can survive and recover, if that is your desire. In order to do this, you must learn to trust God with all that's within you. The longer you live, the more you come to the realization that with God, all things really ARE possible (Matthew 19:26). It is because of God and only God that I am still standing today. After all that He has brought me through, I desire more than ever to become the person He created me to be. I know this is the only way to truly bring glory to His name.

What started on a playground over forty years earlier ended in a pulpit. I guess you could call this my wilderness experience or my forty years of wandering. On the playground, I was in a position of vulnerability but in the pulpit, I am in a position of strength. I am now convinced that God can use ANYTHING to accomplish His purposes. If your life is in a million pieces and you feel you're too messed up to be used by God, YOU ARE WRONG! Those are the ones He's looking for. He's not looking for those who have it all together. The truth of the matter is, none of us do. There are those who pretend to, and that's precisely the problem. Pretense and truth have very little in common.

Once you learn to face reality and to accept God's truth concerning you, it's all uphill from there. You don't have to fight the world's systems to succeed. Promotion comes from God (Psalm 75:6-7) and you will be amazed at how your life will change when you decide to surrender your will, obey God's will for you and trust Him for everything you need.

In the end, there are many who would say that I am not qualified to serve in a ministerial capacity because of all the things I've done. At one time in my life, I would have agreed. Now, I know better. You see, the Bible says before God formed us, He knew us (Jeremiah 1:5). That means He knew all that I would do before I was even born, and decided to call me anyway. Perhaps it is **because** of all that has happened that I am equipped and able to perform the task. It takes strength and courage to overcome adversity. Both these things come from God. In order to gain them, you must present yourself to him in a state of repentance and He will do the rest. I no longer have to seek the approval of man because I have received approval from God. And so have you. Please stop using your past as an excuse to ignore God's call on your life. We are all called to something and our lives cannot be complete until we begin to walk within that calling. Whatever it is that God created you to do comes naturally to you. You get a certain kind of joy and fulfillment from doing it and you would do it whether you were paid for it or not.

Victory comes when you learn to conquer doubt, defeat and fear. When you stop trying to deny what is obviously true, only then can you begin to repair what is wrong in your life. As long as you ignore it, whatever it is remains. When you learn to trust, doubt cannot hinder you any longer. When you embrace victory instead of defeat, the clouds will begin to move away. When you decide to acknowledge and face your fear, it loses its grip on you. You begin to feel larger than life and you start to thrive where you have been planted.

Use these words as permission to take the next step. God has plans for you (Jeremiah 29:11). Dismiss the voice of the enemy and take a bold step in the right direction. God has always been for you and nothing you have done can change His mind. You will never be able to understand the depth of God's love for you but keep trying. Keep allowing that love to push you forward and to inspire you to become all God created you to be.

Lisa Gillespie

Well, it looks like we've come to the end of our time together. As I close this book, I am filled with gratitude for you, the reader. Thank you for hanging in there with me through the good, the bad and everything in between. I hope that your life will be positively impacted by what you have read and that you have been inspired to strive to become the best you that you can possibly be. I hope you now understand that the most important thing you can do in this life is to develop a deep and meaningful relationship with Jesus Christ. He will be everything you need to safely navigate your way through this sin-sick world. He is a gift to you from our Heavenly Father. Receive the gift.

As a final thought, I leave you with this prayer:

Gracious God our Heavenly Father, bless the person who is reading these words right now. Forgive them of their sins and cleanse them from all unrighteousness. Allow them the opportunity to know You in an intimate and personal way. Touch their life with the blessings of peace and power. Deliver them from every stronghold that has or is attempting to manifest in their lives. Cancel the plan of the enemy over this person right now, in the Name of Jesus. Set them free to do Your will. Make what seems to be impossible, possible. Give them the strength and courage to obey Your Word, that their life will become a reflection of Your goodness, grace and glory. This is my prayer, in Jesus' Name, Amen!

Lisa Gillespie

About The Author

Lisa Gillespie was born and raised in Washington, DC. She currently serves in a ministerial capacity at the Hope Fellowship Christian Church in northeast Washington and the Greater Rock Creek Baptist Church in Mt. Rainier, Maryland. She especially enjoys ministry activities involving the empowerment of women and caring for the elderly. She speaks at women's conferences, churches and retreats and lives in Prince George's County, Maryland.

If this book has encouraged you in any way, Lisa would love to hear from you. You may contact her at:

P.O. Box 4171
Washington, DC 20044

Or at the following email address:

lisagillespieministries@gmail.com

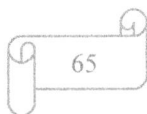

Lisa Gillespie

About Kingdom Journey Press

Kingdom Journey Press, Inc. is a full-service publishing company specializing in providing customized services to support our clients from the conception of an idea to getting HIStory to the masses! Since the time of inception and in conjunction with our umbrella organization, Kingdom Journey Enterprises, we have become recognized globally for our ability to establish a unique presence, while building relationships with partners and clients consisting of current and aspiring writers, and ministry, business, and community organizations.

Our services include:

- ❖ Manuscript Evaluation
- ❖ Coaching for current and aspiring authors
- ❖ Editing
- ❖ Cover and Print Layout Design
- ❖ Print and E-Book Format
- ❖ Copyright and Distribution
- ❖ Marketing and Sales Support

For more information, visit our website at www.kjpressinc.com.

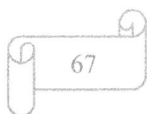

Lisa Gillespie